## This Journal Belongs to:

_____

_____

_____

# Garden Planner and Log Book

*Monthly Gardening Organizer Notebook for Avid Gardeners,*
*Flowers, Vegetable Growing, Plants Profiles and Layout Design*

All rights reserved. No part of this publication may be reproduced without the prior permission of the copyright owner.

© Copyright 2023 by Perigee Trade

Contact us: perigeetrade@proton.me

Plant Name:_____

Date Planted:_____

Purchased at:_____

Price:_____

◯ Seed    ◯ Transplant

Picture

Water: 💧 💧💧 💧💧💧

Sunlight: ☀ ☼ ●

| Date | Event |
|---|---|
|  |  |
|  |  |
|  |  |
|  |  |
|  |  |
|  |  |
|  |  |

Notes: _____
_____
_____
_____

Outcome

Uses

Plant Name:_____

Date Planted:_____

Purchased at:_____

Price:_____

○ Seed    ○ Transplant

Picture

Water: 💧 💧💧 💧💧💧

Sunlight: ☼ ☼ ●

| Date | Event |
|------|-------|
|      |       |
|      |       |
|      |       |
|      |       |
|      |       |
|      |       |
|      |       |

Notes: _____
_____
_____
_____

Outcome

Uses

Plant Name:_____

Date Planted:_____

Purchased at:_____

Price:_____

◯ Seed          ◯ Transplant

Picture

Water: 💧 💧💧 💧💧💧

Sunlight: ☀︎ ☼ ●

| Date | Event |
|------|-------|
|      |       |
|      |       |
|      |       |
|      |       |
|      |       |
|      |       |
|      |       |

Notes: _____
_____
_____
_____

Outcome

Uses

Plant Name:_____

Date Planted:_____

Purchased at:_____

Price:_____

◯ Seed        ◯ Transplant

Picture

Water: 💧 💧💧 💧💧💧

Sunlight: ☀ ☼ ●

| Date | Event |
|------|-------|
|      |       |
|      |       |
|      |       |
|      |       |
|      |       |
|      |       |
|      |       |

Notes: _____
_____
_____
_____

Outcome

Uses

Plant Name: _____

Date Planted: _____

Purchased at: _____

Price: _____

◯ Seed  ◯ Transplant

Picture

Water: 💧 💧💧 💧💧💧

Sunlight: ☀ ☀ ●

| Date | Event |
|------|-------|
|      |       |
|      |       |
|      |       |
|      |       |
|      |       |
|      |       |
|      |       |

Notes: _____
_____
_____
_____

Outcome

Uses

Plant Name:_____

Date Planted:_____

Purchased at:_____

Price:_____

◯ Seed     ◯ Transplant

Picture

Water: 💧 💧💧 💧💧💧

Sunlight: ☀ ☀ ●

| Date | Event |
|---|---|
|  |  |
|  |  |
|  |  |
|  |  |
|  |  |
|  |  |
|  |  |

Notes: _____
_____
_____
_____

Outcome

Uses

Plant Name:_____

Date Planted:_____

Purchased at:_____

Price:_____

◯ Seed    ◯ Transplant

Picture

Water: 💧 💧💧 💧💧💧

Sunlight: ☀ ☼ ●

| Date | Event |
|---|---|
|  |  |
|  |  |
|  |  |
|  |  |
|  |  |
|  |  |
|  |  |

Notes: _____
_____
_____
_____

Outcome

Uses

Plant Name:_____

Date Planted:_____

Purchased at:_____

Price:_____

◯ Seed    ◯ Transplant

Picture

Water: 💧 💧💧 💧💧💧

Sunlight: ☀ ☀ ●

| Date | Event |
|------|-------|
|      |       |
|      |       |
|      |       |
|      |       |
|      |       |
|      |       |
|      |       |

Notes: _____
_____
_____
_____

Outcome

Uses

Plant Name:_____

Date Planted:_____

Purchased at:_____

Price:_____

○ Seed     ○ Transplant

Picture

Water: 💧 💧💧 💧💧💧

Sunlight: ☀ ☀ ●

| Date | Event |
|------|-------|
|      |       |
|      |       |
|      |       |
|      |       |
|      |       |
|      |       |
|      |       |

Notes: _____
_____
_____
_____

Outcome

Uses

Plant Name:_____

Date Planted:_____

Purchased at:_____

Price:_____

◯ Seed    ◯ Transplant

Picture

Water: 💧 💧💧 💧💧💧

Sunlight: ☀ ☀ ●

| Date | Event |
|---|---|
|  |  |
|  |  |
|  |  |
|  |  |
|  |  |
|  |  |
|  |  |

Notes: _____
_____
_____
_____

Outcome

Uses

Plant Name:_____

Date Planted:_____

Purchased at:_____

Price:_____

◯ Seed      ◯ Transplant

Picture

Water: 💧 💧💧 💧💧💧

Sunlight: ☀ ☼ ●

| Date | Event |
|---|---|
|  |  |
|  |  |
|  |  |
|  |  |
|  |  |
|  |  |
|  |  |

Notes: _____
_____
_____
_____

Outcome

Uses

Plant Name:_____

Date Planted:_____

Purchased at:_____

Price:_____

○ Seed        ○ Transplant

Picture

Water: 💧 💧💧 💧💧💧

Sunlight: ☀ ☀ ●

| Date | Event |
|---|---|
|  |  |
|  |  |
|  |  |
|  |  |
|  |  |
|  |  |
|  |  |

Notes: _____
_____
_____
_____

Outcome

Uses

Plant Name:_____

Date Planted:_____

Purchased at:_____

Price:_____

◯ Seed    ◯ Transplant

Picture

Water: 💧 💧💧 💧💧💧

Sunlight: ☀ ☀ ●

| Date | Event |
|---|---|
|  |  |
|  |  |
|  |  |
|  |  |
|  |  |
|  |  |
|  |  |
|  |  |

Notes: _____
_____
_____
_____

Outcome

Uses

Plant Name: _____

Date Planted: _____

Purchased at: _____

Price: _____

◯ Seed        ◯ Transplant

Picture

Water: 💧 💧💧 💧💧💧

Sunlight: ☀ ☼ ●

| Date | Event |
|------|-------|
|      |       |
|      |       |
|      |       |
|      |       |
|      |       |
|      |       |
|      |       |

Notes: _____
_____
_____
_____

Outcome

Uses

Plant Name: _____

Date Planted: _____

Purchased at: _____

Price: _____

◯ Seed     ◯ Transplant

Picture

Water: 💧 💧💧 💧💧💧

Sunlight: ☀ ☼ ●

| Date | Event |
|---|---|
|  |  |
|  |  |
|  |  |
|  |  |
|  |  |
|  |  |
|  |  |
|  |  |

Notes: _____
_____
_____
_____

Outcome

Uses

Plant Name:_____

Date Planted:_____

Purchased at:_____

Price:_____

◯ Seed    ◯ Transplant

Picture

Water: 💧 💧💧 💧💧💧

Sunlight: ☀ ☀ ●

| Date | Event |
|---|---|
|  |  |
|  |  |
|  |  |
|  |  |
|  |  |
|  |  |
|  |  |

Notes: _____
_____
_____
_____

Outcome

Uses

Plant Name:_____

Date Planted:_____

Purchased at:_____

Price:_____

◯ Seed    ◯ Transplant

Picture

Water: 💧 💧💧 💧💧💧

Sunlight: ☀ ☾ ●

| Date | Event |
|------|-------|
|      |       |
|      |       |
|      |       |
|      |       |
|      |       |
|      |       |
|      |       |

Notes: _____
_____
_____
_____

Outcome

Uses

Plant Name:_____

Date Planted:_____

Purchased at:_____

Price:_____

◯ Seed  ◯ Transplant

Picture

Water: 💧 💧💧 💧💧💧

Sunlight: ☀ ☼ ●

| Date | Event |
|------|-------|
|      |       |
|      |       |
|      |       |
|      |       |
|      |       |
|      |       |
|      |       |

Notes: _____
_____
_____
_____

Outcome

Uses

Plant Name:_____

Date Planted:_____

Purchased at:_____

Price:_____

○ Seed    ○ Transplant

Picture

Water: 💧 💧💧 💧💧💧

Sunlight: ☀ ☀ ●

| Date | Event |
|---|---|
|  |  |
|  |  |
|  |  |
|  |  |
|  |  |
|  |  |
|  |  |

Notes: _____
_____
_____
_____

Outcome

Uses

Plant Name: _____

Date Planted: _____

Purchased at: _____

Price: _____

◯ Seed    ◯ Transplant

Picture

Water: 💧 💧💧 💧💧💧

Sunlight: ☀ ☀ ●

| Date | Event |
|---|---|
|  |  |
|  |  |
|  |  |
|  |  |
|  |  |
|  |  |
|  |  |

Notes: _____
_____
_____
_____

Outcome

Uses

Plant Name:_____

Date Planted:_____

Purchased at:_____

Price:_____

◯ Seed    ◯ Transplant

Picture

Water: 💧 💧💧 💧💧💧

Sunlight: ☀ ☀ ●

| Date | Event |
|------|-------|
|      |       |
|      |       |
|      |       |
|      |       |
|      |       |
|      |       |
|      |       |

Notes: _____
_____
_____
_____

Outcome

Uses

Plant Name: _____

Date Planted: _____

Purchased at: _____

Price: _____

◯ Seed    ◯ Transplant

Picture

Water: 💧 💧💧 💧💧💧

Sunlight: ☀ ☼ ●

| Date | Event |
|---|---|
|  |  |
|  |  |
|  |  |
|  |  |
|  |  |
|  |  |
|  |  |

Notes: _____
_____
_____
_____

Outcome

Uses

Plant Name:_____

Date Planted:_____

Purchased at:_____

Price:_____

○ Seed    ○ Transplant

Picture

Water: 💧 💧💧 💧💧💧

Sunlight: ☀ ☼ ●

| Date | Event |
|------|-------|
|      |       |
|      |       |
|      |       |
|      |       |
|      |       |
|      |       |
|      |       |

Notes: _____
_____
_____
_____

Outcome

Uses

Plant Name:_____

Date Planted:_____

Purchased at:_____

Price:_____

◯ Seed      ◯ Transplant

Picture

Water: 💧 💧💧 💧💧💧

Sunlight: ☀ ☀ ●

| Date | Event |
|------|-------|
|      |       |
|      |       |
|      |       |
|      |       |
|      |       |
|      |       |
|      |       |

Notes: _____
_____
_____
_____

Outcome

Uses

Plant Name:_____

Date Planted:_____

Purchased at:_____

Price:_____

○ Seed      ○ Transplant

Water: 💧 💧💧 💧💧💧

Sunlight: ☀ ☀ ●

| Date | Event |
|---|---|
|  |  |
|  |  |
|  |  |
|  |  |
|  |  |
|  |  |
|  |  |

Notes: _____
_____
_____
_____

Outcome

Uses

Plant Name:_____

Date Planted:_____

Purchased at:_____

Price:_____

○ Seed     ○ Transplant

Picture

Water: 💧 💧💧 💧💧💧

Sunlight: ☼ ☼ ●

| Date | Event |
|------|-------|
|      |       |
|      |       |
|      |       |
|      |       |
|      |       |
|      |       |
|      |       |

Notes: _____
_____
_____
_____

Outcome

Uses

Plant Name:_____

Date Planted:_____

Purchased at:_____

Price:_____

○ Seed        ○ Transplant

Picture

Water: 💧 💧💧 💧💧💧

Sunlight: ☀ ☀ ⬤

| Date | Event |
|------|-------|
|      |       |
|      |       |
|      |       |
|      |       |
|      |       |
|      |       |
|      |       |

Notes: _____
_____
_____
_____

Outcome

Uses

Plant Name:_____

Date Planted:_____

Purchased at:_____

Price:_____

◯ Seed      ◯ Transplant

Picture

Water: 💧 💧💧 💧💧💧

Sunlight: ☀ ☼ ●

| Date | Event |
|------|-------|
|      |       |
|      |       |
|      |       |
|      |       |
|      |       |
|      |       |
|      |       |

Notes: _____
_____
_____
_____

Outcome

Uses

Plant Name: _____

Date Planted: _____

Purchased at: _____

Price: _____

◯ Seed    ◯ Transplant

Picture

Water: 💧 💧💧 💧💧💧

Sunlight: ☀ ☼ ●

| Date | Event |
|---|---|
|  |  |
|  |  |
|  |  |
|  |  |
|  |  |
|  |  |
|  |  |
|  |  |

Notes: _____
_____
_____
_____

Outcome

Uses

Plant Name:_____

Date Planted:_____

Purchased at:_____

Price:_____

○ Seed     ○ Transplant

Picture

Water: 💧 💧💧 💧💧💧

Sunlight: ☀️ 🌤 ●

| Date | Event |
|---|---|
|  |  |
|  |  |
|  |  |
|  |  |
|  |  |
|  |  |
|  |  |

Notes: _____
_____
_____
_____

Outcome

Uses

Plant Name:_____

Date Planted:_____

Purchased at:_____

Price:_____

◯ Seed    ◯ Transplant

Picture

Water: 💧 💧💧 💧💧💧

Sunlight: ☀ ⛅ ●

| Date | Event |
|---|---|
|  |  |
|  |  |
|  |  |
|  |  |
|  |  |
|  |  |
|  |  |

Notes: _____
_____
_____
_____

Outcome

Uses

Plant Name: _____

Date Planted: _____

Purchased at: _____

Price: _____

◯ Seed      ◯ Transplant

Picture

Water: 💧 💧💧 💧💧💧

Sunlight: ☀ 🌤 ●

| Date | Event |
|------|-------|
|      |       |
|      |       |
|      |       |
|      |       |
|      |       |
|      |       |
|      |       |

Notes: _____
_____
_____
_____

Outcome

Uses

Plant Name:_____

Date Planted:_____

Purchased at:_____

Price:_____

◯ Seed   ◯ Transplant

Picture

Water: 💧 💧💧 💧💧💧

Sunlight: ☀ ☀ ●

| Date | Event |
|---|---|
|  |  |
|  |  |
|  |  |
|  |  |
|  |  |
|  |  |
|  |  |

Notes: _____
_____
_____
_____

Outcome

Uses

Plant Name:_____

Date Planted:_____

Purchased at:_____

Price:_____

◯ Seed  ◯ Transplant

Picture

Water: 💧 💧💧 💧💧💧

Sunlight: ☀ ☼ ●

| Date | Event |
|---|---|
|  |  |
|  |  |
|  |  |
|  |  |
|  |  |
|  |  |
|  |  |

Notes: _____
_____
_____
_____

Outcome

Uses

Plant Name:_____

Date Planted:_____

Purchased at:_____

Price:_____

○ Seed      ○ Transplant

Picture

Water: 💧 💧💧 💧💧💧

Sunlight: ☀ ☼ ●

| Date | Event |
|------|-------|
|      |       |
|      |       |
|      |       |
|      |       |
|      |       |
|      |       |
|      |       |
|      |       |

Notes: _____
_____
_____
_____

Outcome

Uses

Plant Name:_____

Date Planted:_____

Purchased at:_____

Price:_____

◯ Seed     ◯ Transplant

Picture

Water: 💧 💧💧 💧💧💧

Sunlight: ☀ ☼ ●

| Date | Event |
|------|-------|
|      |       |
|      |       |
|      |       |
|      |       |
|      |       |
|      |       |
|      |       |

Notes: _____
_____
_____
_____

Outcome

Uses

Plant Name:_____

Date Planted:_____

Purchased at:_____

Price:_____

◯ Seed　　◯ Transplant

Picture

Water: 💧 💧💧 💧💧💧

Sunlight: ☀ ☀ ●

| Date | Event |
|------|-------|
|      |       |
|      |       |
|      |       |
|      |       |
|      |       |
|      |       |
|      |       |

Notes: _____
_____
_____

Outcome

Uses

Plant Name:_____

Date Planted:_____

Purchased at:_____

Price:_____

◯ Seed     ◯ Transplant

Picture

Water: 💧 💧💧 💧💧💧

Sunlight: ☀ ☼ ●

| Date | Event |
|---|---|
|  |  |
|  |  |
|  |  |
|  |  |
|  |  |
|  |  |
|  |  |

Notes: _____
_____
_____
_____

Outcome

Uses

Plant Name:_____

Date Planted:_____

Purchased at:_____

Price:_____

◯ Seed     ◯ Transplant

Picture

Water: 💧 💧💧 💧💧💧

Sunlight: ☀ ☼ ●

| Date | Event |
|---|---|
|  |  |
|  |  |
|  |  |
|  |  |
|  |  |
|  |  |
|  |  |

Notes: _____
_____
_____
_____

Outcome

Uses

Plant Name:_____

Date Planted:_____

Purchased at:_____

Price:_____

◯ Seed     ◯ Transplant

Picture

Water: 💧 💧💧 💧💧💧

Sunlight: ☀ ☀ ●

| Date | Event |
|------|-------|
|      |       |
|      |       |
|      |       |
|      |       |
|      |       |
|      |       |
|      |       |

Notes: _____
_____
_____
_____

Outcome

Uses

Plant Name:_____

Date Planted:_____

Purchased at:_____

Price:_____

○ Seed         ○ Transplant

Picture

Water: 💧 💧💧 💧💧💧

Sunlight: ☀ ☀ ●

| Date | Event |
|------|-------|
|      |       |
|      |       |
|      |       |
|      |       |
|      |       |
|      |       |
|      |       |

Notes: _____
_____
_____
_____

Outcome

Uses

Plant Name: _____

Date Planted: _____

Purchased at: _____

Price: _____

◯ Seed    ◯ Transplant

Picture

Water: 💧 💧💧 💧💧💧

Sunlight: ☀ ☼ ●

| Date | Event |
|---|---|
|  |  |
|  |  |
|  |  |
|  |  |
|  |  |
|  |  |
|  |  |

Notes: _____
_____
_____
_____

Outcome

Uses

Plant Name:_____

Date Planted:_____

Purchased at:_____

Price:_____

○ Seed     ○ Transplant

Water: 💧 💧💧 💧💧💧     Sunlight: ☀ 🌤 ●

| Date | Event |
|------|-------|
|      |       |
|      |       |
|      |       |
|      |       |
|      |       |
|      |       |
|      |       |

Notes: _____
_____
_____
_____

Outcome

Uses

Plant Name:_____

Date Planted:_____

Purchased at:_____

Price:_____

◯ Seed     ◯ Transplant

Picture

Water: 💧 💧💧 💧💧💧

Sunlight: ☀ ☀ ●

| Date | Event |
|---|---|
|  |  |
|  |  |
|  |  |
|  |  |
|  |  |
|  |  |
|  |  |

Notes: _____
_____
_____
_____

| Outcome | Uses |
|---|---|
|  |  |

Plant Name:_____

Date Planted:_____

Purchased at:_____

Price:_____

◯ Seed   ◯ Transplant

Picture

Water: 💧 💧💧 💧💧💧

Sunlight: ☀ ☀ ⬤

| Date | Event |
|---|---|
|  |  |
|  |  |
|  |  |
|  |  |
|  |  |
|  |  |
|  |  |

Notes: _____
_____
_____
_____

Outcome

Uses

Plant Name: _____

Date Planted: _____

Purchased at: _____

Price: _____

◯ Seed    ◯ Transplant

Picture

Water: 💧 💧💧 💧💧💧

Sunlight: ☀ ☼ ●

| Date | Event |
|---|---|
|  |  |
|  |  |
|  |  |
|  |  |
|  |  |
|  |  |
|  |  |

Notes: _____
_____
_____
_____

Outcome

Uses

Plant Name:_____

Date Planted:_____

Purchased at:_____

Price:_____

◯ Seed    ◯ Transplant

Picture

Water: 💧 💧💧 💧💧💧

Sunlight: ☀ ☀ ●

| Date | Event |
|---|---|
|  |  |
|  |  |
|  |  |
|  |  |
|  |  |
|  |  |
|  |  |

Notes: _____
_____
_____
_____

Outcome

Uses

Plant Name:_____

Date Planted:_____

Purchased at:_____

Price:_____

◯ Seed    ◯ Transplant

Picture

Water: 💧 💧💧 💧💧💧

Sunlight: ☀ ☼ ●

| Date | Event |
|------|-------|
|      |       |
|      |       |
|      |       |
|      |       |
|      |       |
|      |       |
|      |       |

Notes: _____
_____
_____
_____

Outcome

Uses

Plant Name: _____

Date Planted: _____

Purchased at: _____

Price: _____

○ Seed    ○ Transplant

Picture

Water: 🌢 🌢🌢 🌢🌢🌢

Sunlight: ☀ ☀ ●

| Date | Event |
|------|-------|
|      |       |
|      |       |
|      |       |
|      |       |
|      |       |
|      |       |
|      |       |

Notes: _____
_____
_____
_____

Outcome

Uses

Plant Name:_____

Date Planted:_____

Purchased at:_____

Price:_____

◯ Seed      ◯ Transplant

Picture

Water: 💧 💧💧 💧💧💧

Sunlight: ☀ ☀ ●

| Date | Event |
|---|---|
|  |  |
|  |  |
|  |  |
|  |  |
|  |  |
|  |  |
|  |  |

Notes: _____
_____
_____
_____

Outcome

Uses

Plant Name:_____

Date Planted:_____

Purchased at:_____

Price:_____

○ Seed     ○ Transplant

Picture

Water: 💧 💧💧 💧💧💧

Sunlight: ☀ ☀ ●

| Date | Event |
|------|-------|
|      |       |
|      |       |
|      |       |
|      |       |
|      |       |
|      |       |
|      |       |

Notes: _____
_____
_____
_____

Outcome

Uses

Plant Name:_____

Date Planted:_____

Purchased at:_____

Price:_____

◯ Seed    ◯ Transplant

Picture

Water: 💧 💧💧 💧💧💧

Sunlight: ☀ ☼ ●

| Date | Event |
|---|---|
|  |  |
|  |  |
|  |  |
|  |  |
|  |  |
|  |  |
|  |  |

Notes: _____
_____
_____
_____

Outcome

Uses

Plant Name:_____

Date Planted:_____

Purchased at:_____

Price:_____

◯ Seed          ◯ Transplant

Picture

Water: 💧 💧💧 💧💧💧

Sunlight: ☀ ☀ ●

| Date | Event |
|---|---|
|  |  |
|  |  |
|  |  |
|  |  |
|  |  |
|  |  |
|  |  |

Notes: _____
_____
_____
_____

Outcome

Uses

Plant Name: _____

Date Planted: _____

Purchased at: _____

Price: _____

◯ Seed    ◯ Transplant

Picture

Water: 💧 💧💧 💧💧💧

Sunlight: ☀ ☼ ●

| Date | Event |
|------|-------|
|      |       |
|      |       |
|      |       |
|      |       |
|      |       |
|      |       |
|      |       |

Notes: _____
_____
_____
_____

Outcome

Uses

Plant Name:_____

Date Planted:_____

Purchased at:_____

Price:_____

○ Seed    ○ Transplant

Picture

Water: 💧 💧💧 💧💧💧

Sunlight: ☼ ☼ ●

| Date | Event |
|------|-------|
|      |       |
|      |       |
|      |       |
|      |       |
|      |       |
|      |       |
|      |       |

Notes: _____
_____
_____
_____

Outcome

Uses

Plant Name:_____

Date Planted:_____

Purchased at:_____

Price:_____

○ Seed   ○ Transplant

Picture

Water: 💧 💧💧 💧💧💧

Sunlight: ☀ ☀ ●

| Date | Event |
|---|---|
|  |  |
|  |  |
|  |  |
|  |  |
|  |  |
|  |  |
|  |  |

Notes: _____
_____
_____
_____

Outcome

Uses

Plant Name:_____

Date Planted:_____

Purchased at:_____

Price:_____

◯ Seed     ◯ Transplant

Picture

Water: 💧 💧💧 💧💧💧

Sunlight: ☀ ☀ ●

| Date | Event |
|---|---|
|  |  |
|  |  |
|  |  |
|  |  |
|  |  |
|  |  |
|  |  |

Notes: _____
_____
_____
_____

Outcome

Uses

Plant Name:_____

Date Planted:_____

Purchased at:_____

Price:_____

◯ Seed     ◯ Transplant

Picture

Water: 💧 💧💧 💧💧💧

Sunlight: ☀ ☼ ●

| Date | Event |
|------|-------|
|      |       |
|      |       |
|      |       |
|      |       |
|      |       |
|      |       |
|      |       |

Notes: _____
_____
_____
_____

Outcome

Uses

Plant Name:_____

Date Planted:_____

Purchased at:_____

Price:_____

◯ Seed      ◯ Transplant

Picture

Water: 💧 💧💧 💧💧💧

Sunlight: ☀ ☀ ●

| Date | Event |
|------|-------|
|      |       |
|      |       |
|      |       |
|      |       |
|      |       |
|      |       |
|      |       |

Notes: _____
_____
_____
_____

Outcome

Uses

Plant Name:_____

Date Planted:_____

Purchased at:_____

Price:_____

◯ Seed    ◯ Transplant

Picture

Water: 💧 💧💧 💧💧💧

Sunlight: ☀ ☀ ●

| Date | Event |
|---|---|
|  |  |
|  |  |
|  |  |
|  |  |
|  |  |
|  |  |
|  |  |

Notes: _____
_____
_____
_____

Outcome

Uses

Plant Name:_____

Date Planted:_____

Purchased at:_____

Price:_____

◯ Seed        ◯ Transplant

Picture

Water: 💧 💧💧 💧💧💧

Sunlight: ☀ ☀ ●

| Date | Event |
|------|-------|
|      |       |
|      |       |
|      |       |
|      |       |
|      |       |
|      |       |
|      |       |

Notes: _____
_____
_____
_____

Outcome

Uses

Plant Name:_____

Date Planted:_____

Purchased at:_____

Price:_____

◯ Seed     ◯ Transplant

Picture

Water: 💧 💧💧 💧💧💧

Sunlight: ☀ ☼ ●

| Date | Event |
|------|-------|
|      |       |
|      |       |
|      |       |
|      |       |
|      |       |
|      |       |
|      |       |

Notes: _____
_____
_____
_____

Outcome

Uses

Plant Name:_____

Date Planted:_____

Purchased at:_____

Price:_____

◯ Seed    ◯ Transplant

Picture

Water: 💧 💧💧 💧💧💧

Sunlight: ☀ ☀ ●

| Date | Event |
|------|-------|
|      |       |
|      |       |
|      |       |
|      |       |
|      |       |
|      |       |
|      |       |

Notes: _____
_____
_____
_____

Outcome

Uses

Plant Name: _____

Date Planted: _____

Purchased at: _____

Price: _____

○ Seed       ○ Transplant

Picture

Water: 💧 💧💧 💧💧💧

Sunlight: ☀ ☼ ●

| Date | Event |
|------|-------|
|      |       |
|      |       |
|      |       |
|      |       |
|      |       |
|      |       |
|      |       |

Notes: _____
_____
_____
_____

Outcome

Uses

Plant Name: _____

Date Planted: _____

Purchased at: _____

Price: _____

○ Seed    ○ Transplant

Picture

Water: 💧 💧💧 💧💧💧

Sunlight: ☀ ☀ ●

| Date | Event |
|---|---|
|  |  |
|  |  |
|  |  |
|  |  |
|  |  |
|  |  |
|  |  |

Notes: _____
_____
_____
_____

Outcome

Uses

Plant Name:_____

Date Planted:_____

Purchased at:_____

Price:_____

◯ Seed          ◯ Transplant

Picture

Water: 💧 💧💧 💧💧💧

Sunlight: ☀ ☼ ●

| Date | Event |
|------|-------|
|      |       |
|      |       |
|      |       |
|      |       |
|      |       |
|      |       |
|      |       |

Notes: _____
_____
_____
_____

Outcome

Uses

Plant Name:_____

Date Planted:_____

Purchased at:_____

Price:_____

◯ Seed     ◯ Transplant

Picture

Water: 💧 💧💧 💧💧💧

Sunlight: ☀ ⛅ ●

| Date | Event |
|---|---|
|  |  |
|  |  |
|  |  |
|  |  |
|  |  |
|  |  |
|  |  |

Notes: _____
_____
_____
_____

Outcome

Uses

Plant Name:_____

Date Planted:_____

Purchased at:_____

Price:_____

◯ Seed      ◯ Transplant

Picture

Water: 💧 💧💧 💧💧💧

Sunlight: ☀ ☀ ●

| Date | Event |
|---|---|
|  |  |
|  |  |
|  |  |
|  |  |
|  |  |
|  |  |
|  |  |

Notes: _____
_____
_____
_____

Outcome

Uses

Plant Name:_____

Date Planted:_____

Purchased at:_____

Price:_____

◯ Seed     ◯ Transplant

Picture

Water: 💧 💧💧 💧💧💧

Sunlight: ☀ ☼ ●

| Date | Event |
|---|---|
|  |  |
|  |  |
|  |  |
|  |  |
|  |  |
|  |  |
|  |  |

Notes: _____
_____
_____
_____

Outcome

Uses

Plant Name:_____

Date Planted:_____

Purchased at:_____

Price:_____

◯ Seed    ◯ Transplant

Picture

Water: 💧 💧💧 💧💧💧

Sunlight: ☀ ☼ ●

| Date | Event |
|------|-------|
|      |       |
|      |       |
|      |       |
|      |       |
|      |       |
|      |       |
|      |       |

Notes: _____
_____
_____
_____

Outcome

Uses

Plant Name:_____

Date Planted:_____

Purchased at:_____

Price:_____

◯ Seed    ◯ Transplant

Picture

Water: 💧 💧💧 💧💧💧

Sunlight: ☀ ☀ ●

| Date | Event |
|---|---|
|  |  |
|  |  |
|  |  |
|  |  |
|  |  |
|  |  |
|  |  |

Notes: _____
_____
_____
_____

Outcome

Uses

Plant Name: _____

Date Planted: _____

Purchased at: _____

Price: _____

◯ Seed      ◯ Transplant

Picture

Water: 💧 💧💧 💧💧💧

Sunlight: ☀ ☀ ●

| Date | Event |
|------|-------|
|      |       |
|      |       |
|      |       |
|      |       |
|      |       |
|      |       |
|      |       |

Notes: _____
_____
_____
_____

Outcome

Uses

Plant Name: _____

Date Planted: _____

Purchased at: _____

Price: _____

◯ Seed    ◯ Transplant

Picture

Water: 💧 💧💧 💧💧💧

Sunlight: ☀ ☀ ●

| Date | Event |
|------|-------|
|      |       |
|      |       |
|      |       |
|      |       |
|      |       |
|      |       |
|      |       |

Notes: _____
_____
_____
_____

Outcome

Uses

Plant Name: _____

Date Planted: _____

Purchased at: _____

Price: _____

◯ Seed      ◯ Transplant

Picture

Water: 💧 💧💧 💧💧💧

Sunlight: ☼ ☼ ●

| Date | Event |
|------|-------|
|      |       |
|      |       |
|      |       |
|      |       |
|      |       |
|      |       |
|      |       |

Notes: _____
_____
_____
_____

Outcome

Uses

Plant Name:_____

Date Planted:_____

Purchased at:_____

Price:_____

◯ Seed      ◯ Transplant

Picture

Water: 💧 💧💧 💧💧💧

Sunlight: ☀ ☀ ●

| Date | Event |
|---|---|
|  |  |
|  |  |
|  |  |
|  |  |
|  |  |
|  |  |
|  |  |

Notes: _____
_____
_____
_____

Outcome

Uses

Plant Name:_____

Date Planted:_____

Purchased at:_____

Price:_____

○ Seed          ○ Transplant

Picture

Water: 💧 💧💧 💧💧💧

Sunlight: ☀ ☼ ●

| Date | Event |
|------|-------|
|      |       |
|      |       |
|      |       |
|      |       |
|      |       |
|      |       |
|      |       |

Notes: _____
_____
_____
_____

Outcome

Uses

Plant Name:_____

Date Planted:_____

Purchased at:_____

Price:_____

○ Seed   ○ Transplant

Picture

Water: 💧 💧💧 💧💧💧

Sunlight: ☀ ☀ ●

| Date | Event |
|---|---|
|  |  |
|  |  |
|  |  |
|  |  |
|  |  |
|  |  |
|  |  |

Notes: _____
_____
_____
_____

Outcome

Uses

Plant Name:_____

Date Planted:_____

Purchased at:_____

Price:_____

◯ Seed      ◯ Transplant

Picture

Water: 💧 💧💧 💧💧💧

Sunlight: ☀ ☼ ●

| Date | Event |
|------|-------|
|      |       |
|      |       |
|      |       |
|      |       |
|      |       |
|      |       |
|      |       |

Notes: _____
_____
_____
_____

Outcome

Uses

Plant Name:_____

Date Planted:_____

Purchased at:_____

Price:_____

◯ Seed    ◯ Transplant

Picture

Water: 💧 💧💧 💧💧💧

Sunlight: ☀ ☀ ●

| Date | Event |
|---|---|
|  |  |
|  |  |
|  |  |
|  |  |
|  |  |
|  |  |
|  |  |

Notes: _____
_____
_____
_____

Outcome

Uses

Plant Name: _____

Date Planted: _____

Purchased at: _____

Price: _____

○ Seed  ○ Transplant

Picture

Water: 💧 💧💧 💧💧💧

Sunlight: ☀ ☀ ●

| Date | Event |
|---|---|
|  |  |
|  |  |
|  |  |
|  |  |
|  |  |
|  |  |
|  |  |

Notes: _____
_____
_____
_____

Outcome

Uses

Plant Name:_____

Date Planted:_____

Purchased at:_____

Price:_____

◯ Seed  ◯ Transplant

Picture

Water: 💧 💧💧 💧💧💧

Sunlight: ☀ ☀ ●

| Date | Event |
|---|---|
|  |  |
|  |  |
|  |  |
|  |  |
|  |  |
|  |  |
|  |  |
|  |  |

Notes: _____
_____
_____
_____

Outcome

Uses

Plant Name:_____

Date Planted:_____

Purchased at:_____

Price:_____

◯ Seed     ◯ Transplant

Picture

Water: 💧 💧💧 💧💧💧

Sunlight: ☀ ☼ ●

| Date | Event |
|------|-------|
|      |       |
|      |       |
|      |       |
|      |       |
|      |       |
|      |       |
|      |       |

Notes: _____
_____
_____
_____

Outcome

Uses

Plant Name:_____

Date Planted:_____

Purchased at:_____

Price:_____

◯ Seed     ◯ Transplant

Picture

Water: 💧 💧💧 💧💧💧

Sunlight: ☀ ☼ ●

| Date | Event |
|---|---|
|  |  |
|  |  |
|  |  |
|  |  |
|  |  |
|  |  |
|  |  |

Notes: _____
_____
_____
_____

Outcome

Uses

Plant Name:_____

Date Planted:_____

Purchased at:_____

Price:_____

◯ Seed      ◯ Transplant

Picture

Water: 💧 💧💧 💧💧💧

Sunlight: ☀ ☀ ●

| Date | Event |
|------|-------|
|      |       |
|      |       |
|      |       |
|      |       |
|      |       |
|      |       |
|      |       |

Notes: _____
_____
_____
_____

Outcome

Uses

Plant Name:_____

Date Planted:_____

Purchased at:_____

Price:_____

◯ Seed ◯ Transplant

Picture

Water: 💧 💧💧 💧💧💧

Sunlight: ☀ ☀ ●

| Date | Event |
|---|---|
|  |  |
|  |  |
|  |  |
|  |  |
|  |  |
|  |  |
|  |  |

Notes: _____
_____
_____
_____

Outcome

Uses

Plant Name: _____

Date Planted: _____

Purchased at: _____

Price: _____

○ Seed   ○ Transplant

Picture

Water: 💧 💧💧 💧💧💧

Sunlight: ☀ ☼ ●

| Date | Event |
|------|-------|
|      |       |
|      |       |
|      |       |
|      |       |
|      |       |
|      |       |
|      |       |

Notes: _____
_____
_____
_____

Outcome

Uses

Plant Name:_____

Date Planted:_____

Purchased at:_____

Price:_____

◯ Seed    ◯ Transplant

Picture

Water: 💧 💧💧 💧💧💧

Sunlight: ☀ ☀ ⬤

| Date | Event |
|------|-------|
|      |       |
|      |       |
|      |       |
|      |       |
|      |       |
|      |       |
|      |       |

Notes: _____
_____
_____
_____

Outcome

Uses

Plant Name:_____

Date Planted:_____

Purchased at:_____

Price:_____

◯ Seed    ◯ Transplant

Picture

Water: 💧 💧💧 💧💧💧

Sunlight: ☀ ☽ ●

| Date | Event |
|---|---|
|  |  |
|  |  |
|  |  |
|  |  |
|  |  |
|  |  |
|  |  |

Notes: _____
_____
_____
_____

| Outcome | Uses |
|---|---|
|  |  |

Plant Name: _____

Date Planted: _____

Purchased at: _____

Price: _____

○ Seed    ○ Transplant

Picture

Water: 💧 💧💧 💧💧💧

Sunlight: ☀ ☼ ●

| Date | Event |
|------|-------|
|      |       |
|      |       |
|      |       |
|      |       |
|      |       |
|      |       |
|      |       |

Notes: _____
_____
_____
_____

Outcome

Uses

Plant Name:_____

Date Planted:_____

Purchased at:_____

Price:_____

◯ Seed     ◯ Transplant

Picture

Water: 💧 💧💧 💧💧💧

Sunlight: ☀ ☀ ●

| Date | Event |
|------|-------|
|      |       |
|      |       |
|      |       |
|      |       |
|      |       |
|      |       |
|      |       |

Notes: _____
_____
_____
_____

Outcome

Uses

Plant Name:_____

Date Planted:_____

Purchased at:_____

Price:_____

◯ Seed      ◯ Transplant

Picture

Water: 💧 💧💧 💧💧💧

Sunlight: ☀ ☀ ●

| Date | Event |
|---|---|
|  |  |
|  |  |
|  |  |
|  |  |
|  |  |
|  |  |
|  |  |

Notes: _____
_____
_____
_____

Outcome

Uses

Plant Name:_____

Date Planted:_____

Purchased at:_____

Price:_____

◯ Seed    ◯ Transplant

Picture

Water: 💧 💧💧 💧💧💧

Sunlight: ☀ ☼ ●

| Date | Event |
|------|-------|
|      |       |
|      |       |
|      |       |
|      |       |
|      |       |
|      |       |
|      |       |

Notes: _____
_____
_____
_____

Outcome

Uses

Plant Name:_____

Date Planted:_____

Purchased at:_____

Price:_____

◯ Seed        ◯ Transplant

Picture

Water: 💧 💧💧 💧💧💧

Sunlight: ☀ ☼ ●

| Date | Event |
|------|-------|
|      |       |
|      |       |
|      |       |
|      |       |
|      |       |
|      |       |
|      |       |

Notes: _____
_____
_____
_____

Outcome

Uses

Plant Name:_____

Date Planted:_____

Purchased at:_____

Price:_____

○ Seed     ○ Transplant

Picture

Water: 💧 💧💧 💧💧💧

Sunlight: ☀ ☀ ●

| Date | Event |
|---|---|
|  |  |
|  |  |
|  |  |
|  |  |
|  |  |
|  |  |
|  |  |

Notes: _____
_____
_____
_____

Outcome

Uses

Plant Name:_____

Date Planted:_____

Purchased at:_____

Price:_____

◯ Seed        ◯ Transplant

Picture

Water: 💧 💧💧 💧💧💧

Sunlight: ☀ ☀ ●

| Date | Event |
|------|-------|
|      |       |
|      |       |
|      |       |
|      |       |
|      |       |
|      |       |
|      |       |

Notes: _____
_____
_____
_____

Outcome

Uses

Plant Name:_____

Date Planted:_____

Purchased at:_____

Price:_____

◯ Seed    ◯ Transplant

Picture

Water: 💧 💧💧 💧💧💧

Sunlight: ☀ 🌤 ●

| Date | Event |
|---|---|
|  |  |
|  |  |
|  |  |
|  |  |
|  |  |
|  |  |
|  |  |

Notes: _____
_____
_____
_____

Outcome

Uses

Plant Name:_____

Date Planted:_____

Purchased at:_____

Price:_____

○ Seed　　　○ Transplant

Picture

Water:

Sunlight:

| Date | Event |
|---|---|
|  |  |
|  |  |
|  |  |
|  |  |
|  |  |
|  |  |
|  |  |

Notes: _____
_____
_____
_____

Outcome

Uses

Plant Name:_____

Date Planted:_____

Purchased at:_____

Price:_____

◯ Seed    ◯ Transplant

Picture

Water: 💧 💧💧 💧💧💧

Sunlight: ☀ ☼ ●

| Date | Event |
|------|-------|
|      |       |
|      |       |
|      |       |
|      |       |
|      |       |
|      |       |
|      |       |

Notes: _____
_____
_____
_____

Outcome

Uses

Plant Name:_____

Date Planted:_____

Purchased at:_____

Price:_____

◯ Seed    ◯ Transplant

Picture

Water: 💧 💧💧 💧💧💧

Sunlight: ☀ ☼ ●

| Date | Event |
|---|---|
|  |  |
|  |  |
|  |  |
|  |  |
|  |  |
|  |  |
|  |  |

Notes: _____
_____
_____
_____

Outcome

Uses